EMMANUEL JOSEPH

The Mind's Machine, How Philosophy and Technology Have Redefined Human History

Copyright © 2025 by Emmanuel Joseph

All rights reserved. No part of this publication may be reproduced, stored or transmitted in any form or by any means, electronic, mechanical, photocopying, recording, scanning, or otherwise without written permission from the publisher. It is illegal to copy this book, post it to a website, or distribute it by any other means without permission.

First edition

This book was professionally typeset on Reedsy.
Find out more at reedsy.com

Contents

1	Chapter 1: The Dawn of Thought	1
2	Chapter 2: Ancient Philosophers	3
3	Chapter 3: The Renaissance Awakening	5
4	Chapter 4: The Age of Enlightenment	7
5	Chapter 5: The Industrial Revolution	9
6	Chapter 6: The Rise of Modern Philosophy	11
7	Chapter 7: The Digital Revolution	13
8	Chapter 8: Artificial Intelligence	15
9	Chapter 9: Biotechnology	17
10	Chapter 10: Space Exploration	19
11	Chapter 11: Environmental Philosophy	21
12	Chapter 12: Transhumanism	23
13	Chapter 13: The Philosophy of Technology	25
14	Chapter 14: The Future of Human Thought	28
15	Chapter 15: Conclusion: The Mind's Machine	30

1

Chapter 1: The Dawn of Thought

From the earliest days of humanity, the first flicker of thought ignited a revolution. As humans began to question their existence, the seeds of philosophy were sown. These primitive contemplations evolved into sophisticated systems of thought, shaping early societies and their relationship with the natural world. The inception of human cognition was marked by the development of language, a tool that enabled abstract thinking and complex communication. Early humans used symbols and sounds to convey ideas, laying the foundation for philosophical discourse.

As societies formed, so did the need to explain the world around them. Myths and legends emerged as the first attempts to make sense of existence. These stories were not mere tales but represented the collective wisdom and philosophical insights of early cultures. They provided answers to fundamental questions about life, death, and the cosmos. Over time, these mythological narratives evolved into more structured philosophical systems, influencing the development of ethics, politics, and metaphysics.

In ancient Mesopotamia and Egypt, the earliest records of human thought can be found in cuneiform tablets and hieroglyphic inscriptions. These civilizations developed complex cosmologies and ethical codes, reflecting their understanding of the world. The Sumerians, for example, created the "Enuma Elish," a creation myth that explored the origins of the universe and the role of gods in shaping human destiny. Similarly, the Egyptians believed in Ma'at, the concept of truth, balance, and order, which guided their moral and social conduct.

The evolution of human thought was further accelerated by the interaction between different cultures. As civilizations expanded and traded, they exchanged ideas and philosophies. This cross-cultural exchange enriched human understanding and led to the development of more diverse and complex philosophical systems. The ancient Greeks, for instance, were heavily influenced by Egyptian and Mesopotamian thought, which laid the groundwork for their own philosophical inquiries. Thus, the dawn of thought was not a solitary event but a collective endeavor that spanned across continents and millennia.

Now let's move on to Chapter 2.

2

Chapter 2: Ancient Philosophers

The ancient world was a cauldron of intellectual exploration. From Socrates and Plato in Greece to Confucius in China, great minds sought to unravel the mysteries of existence. Their ideas about ethics, politics, and the cosmos laid the groundwork for future intellectual pursuits. The Greeks, in particular, were pioneers in the field of philosophy, developing schools of thought that still resonate today.

Socrates, often regarded as the father of Western philosophy, challenged conventional wisdom through his method of questioning. His dialectical approach, known as the Socratic method, encouraged critical thinking and self-examination. Socrates' insistence on questioning everything led to his trial and execution, but his ideas lived on through his students, most notably Plato. Plato's writings, including "The Republic," explored concepts of justice, the ideal state, and the nature of reality. His theory of forms proposed that the material world is a shadow of a higher, immutable realm of ideas.

Aristotle, Plato's student, took a more empirical approach to philosophy. He believed that knowledge could be gained through observation and experience. Aristotle's works covered a wide range of subjects, from ethics and politics to biology and metaphysics. His Nicomachean Ethics introduced the concept of the "Golden Mean," advocating for a balanced and virtuous life. Aristotle's influence extended beyond philosophy, shaping the development of Western science and logic.

Meanwhile, in the East, Confucius laid the foundation for Chinese philosophy. His teachings focused on morality, social harmony, and the importance of education. Confucius emphasized the values of filial piety, respect for elders, and the cultivation of virtuous character. His ideas were compiled by his disciples in the "Analects," a collection of sayings and dialogues that became the cornerstone of Confucian thought. Confucius' influence permeated Chinese society, shaping its cultural and political institutions for centuries.

These ancient philosophers were not isolated thinkers but part of larger intellectual traditions. Their ideas interacted with and influenced one another, creating a rich tapestry of thought. The legacies of Socrates, Plato, Aristotle, and Confucius continue to shape our understanding of the world and our place in it. Their inquiries into the nature of existence, ethics, and society laid the groundwork for future philosophical explorations and technological advancements.

3

Chapter 3: The Renaissance Awakening

The Renaissance marked a profound shift in human history. As Europe emerged from the Dark Ages, a renewed interest in classical philosophy and art sparked a cultural rebirth. This era saw the fusion of ancient wisdom with new scientific discoveries, challenging established beliefs and redefining human potential. The Renaissance was characterized by a spirit of curiosity and innovation, which propelled advancements in art, science, and literature.

One of the most significant figures of the Renaissance was Leonardo da Vinci. A polymath whose interests spanned painting, anatomy, engineering, and astronomy, Leonardo embodied the Renaissance ideal of the "universal man." His masterpieces, such as the "Mona Lisa" and "The Last Supper," revolutionized the art world with their use of perspective and human emotion. Leonardo's notebooks, filled with sketches and scientific observations, reveal his relentless quest for knowledge and understanding.

Meanwhile, the invention of the printing press by Johannes Gutenberg in the mid-15th century transformed the dissemination of knowledge. This groundbreaking technology made books more accessible, allowing ideas to spread rapidly across Europe. The proliferation of printed materials facilitated the exchange of philosophical and scientific ideas, fueling the intellectual fervor of the Renaissance. Figures like Niccolò Machiavelli and Thomas More used the printed word to explore political theory and social reform, challenging traditional notions of governance and ethics.

The Renaissance also witnessed the birth of modern science. Nicolaus Copernicus, Galileo Galilei, and Johannes Kepler made groundbreaking discoveries that challenged the geocentric model of the universe. Their work laid the foundation for the Scientific Revolution, a period of unprecedented advancements in mathematics, physics, and astronomy. These scientific pioneers employed empirical methods and rigorous observation, breaking away from the Aristotelian scholasticism that had dominated medieval thought.

The fusion of art, science, and philosophy during the Renaissance led to a deeper understanding of the human condition and the natural world. This era's emphasis on individualism and critical thinking laid the groundwork for the Enlightenment and the modern age. The Renaissance awakening was not just a revival of classical antiquity but a transformative period that reshaped the trajectory of human history.

Now let's continue with Chapter 4.

4

Chapter 4: The Age of Enlightenment

The Enlightenment was a period of intellectual liberation. Thinkers like Voltaire, Rousseau, and Kant championed reason, individualism, and skepticism of authority. Their ideas catalyzed political revolutions and advanced scientific progress, reshaping societies across the globe. The Enlightenment was driven by the belief that human reason could overcome ignorance and tyranny, paving the way for a more just and equitable world.

Voltaire, a prolific writer and philosopher, was a fierce advocate for freedom of speech and religious tolerance. His satirical works, such as "Candide," criticized the dogmas and injustices of his time. Voltaire's emphasis on reason and critical thinking inspired future generations to challenge authoritarianism and advocate for civil liberties. His wit and eloquence made him a leading figure of the Enlightenment, and his ideas continue to influence contemporary debates on human rights and social justice.

Jean-Jacques Rousseau, another key Enlightenment thinker, explored the relationship between individuals and society. In his seminal work, "The Social Contract," Rousseau argued that legitimate political authority arises from the collective will of the people. He believed that individuals are born free but are constrained by societal institutions. Rousseau's ideas on democracy, education, and personal freedom had a profound impact on the development of modern political thought and the French Revolution.

Immanuel Kant, a German philosopher, sought to reconcile rationalism and empiricism. His "Critique of Pure Reason" explored the limits of human knowledge and the nature of reality. Kant's philosophy emphasized the importance of autonomy and moral duty, arguing that individuals should act according to universal principles. His ideas on ethics, epistemology, and metaphysics laid the foundation for modern philosophy and continue to shape contemporary debates in various fields.

The Enlightenment also saw significant advancements in science and technology. Figures like Isaac Newton and Carl Linnaeus made groundbreaking discoveries in physics and biology, respectively. Newton's laws of motion and universal gravitation revolutionized the understanding of the natural world, while Linnaeus' classification system provided a framework for organizing biological diversity. These scientific achievements were fueled by the Enlightenment's emphasis on empirical observation and rational inquiry.

The Age of Enlightenment was a transformative period that reshaped human thought and society. The era's emphasis on reason, individualism, and skepticism of authority challenged traditional beliefs and paved the way for political, social, and scientific advancements. The intellectual legacy of the Enlightenment continues to influence contemporary thought and guide humanity's quest for knowledge and progress.

5

Chapter 5: The Industrial Revolution

The Industrial Revolution was a technological tsunami that redefined human life. Innovations in machinery, transportation, and communication fueled unprecedented economic growth and urbanization. However, this era also brought about social upheaval and environmental challenges. The Industrial Revolution transformed society in profound ways, laying the groundwork for the modern world.

One of the most significant advancements of the Industrial Revolution was the development of steam power. The steam engine, invented by James Watt, revolutionized transportation and manufacturing. Steam-powered locomotives and ships enabled faster and more efficient movement of goods and people, facilitating global trade and exploration. Factories powered by steam engines increased production capacity, leading to the mass production of goods and the rise of industrial cities.

The invention of the spinning jenny and the power loom revolutionized the textile industry. These machines automated the process of spinning and weaving, increasing efficiency and reducing the need for manual labor. The textile industry became a driving force of the Industrial Revolution, contributing to economic growth and the rise of consumer culture. However, the shift to industrial production also led to harsh working conditions and the exploitation of labor, particularly for women and children.

The Industrial Revolution also saw significant advancements in communication. The invention of the telegraph by Samuel Morse revolutionized long-distance communication, enabling instant transmission of messages across vast distances. The telegraph network facilitated the coordination of business activities, the dissemination of news, and the management of transportation systems. This era also witnessed the birth of the modern postal system and the development of mass media, transforming how information was shared and consumed.

The rapid industrialization and urbanization of the Industrial Revolution brought about significant social and environmental challenges. The rise of factory work led to the migration of people from rural areas to urban centers, resulting in overcrowded and unsanitary living conditions. The exploitation of labor and the lack of workers' rights sparked social movements and labor reforms. Additionally, the increased use of fossil fuels and the expansion of industrial activities contributed to environmental degradation and pollution.

The Industrial Revolution was a period of immense technological and social change that reshaped human society. The innovations of this era laid the foundation for modern industrial economies and transformed the way people lived and worked. While the Industrial Revolution brought about significant progress, it also highlighted the need for ethical considerations and social responsibility in the face of rapid technological advancement.

6

Chapter 6: The Rise of Modern Philosophy

The 19th and 20th centuries witnessed a proliferation of philosophical movements. From existentialism to pragmatism, new schools of thought emerged in response to the rapidly changing world. These philosophies grappled with the complexities of human existence in an age of technological progress. The rise of modern philosophy reflected the evolving concerns and aspirations of humanity.

Existentialism, a philosophical movement that emerged in the 19th century, explored themes of individual freedom, choice, and the search for meaning. Pioneered by thinkers such as Søren Kierkegaard and Friedrich Nietzsche, existentialism challenged traditional notions of objective truth and emphasized the importance of personal experience. Kierkegaard's exploration of faith and despair and Nietzsche's critique of morality and the concept of the "Übermensch" influenced existentialist thought. In the 20th century, existentialism gained prominence through the works of Jean-Paul Sartre and Simone de Beauvoir, who examined issues of identity, freedom, and responsibility.

Pragmatism, another influential philosophical movement, emerged in the United States in the late 19th century. Founded by Charles Sanders Peirce, William James, and John Dewey, pragmatism focused on the practical consequences of ideas and the value of beliefs in guiding action. Pragmatists argued that truth is not a fixed, absolute concept but is instead determined by its usefulness and applicability in real-life situations. This emphasis on practical problem-solving and experimentation had a significant impact on American education, politics, and social reform.

The rise of modern philosophy also saw the development of analytic philosophy, which emphasized clarity, logic, and linguistic analysis. Thinkers such as Bertrand Russell, Ludwig Wittgenstein, and G.E. Moore sought to address philosophical problems through rigorous logical analysis and the examination of language. Analytic philosophy became the dominant approach in the Anglo-American philosophical tradition, shaping the discourse in areas such as philosophy of mind, epistemology, and ethics.

Continental philosophy, on the other hand, encompassed a diverse range of movements and thinkers in Europe. Phenomenology, developed by Edmund Husserl and expanded by Martin Heidegger, focused on the study of conscious experience and the structures of perception. Critical theory, associated with the Frankfurt School, examined the relationship between society, culture, and power, critiquing the ideologies that perpetuate social inequalities. Poststructuralism and deconstruction, represented by thinkers like Michel Foucault and Jacques Derrida, challenged traditional assumptions about language, identity, and knowledge.

The rise of modern philosophy reflected the dynamic and multifaceted nature of human thought in response to a rapidly changing world. These philosophical movements addressed the complexities of existence, knowledge, and ethics in an age of technological progress and social transformation. The ideas and debates of modern philosophy continue to shape contemporary discourse and inform our understanding of the human condition.

7

Chapter 7: The Digital Revolution

The advent of computers and the internet heralded the Digital Revolution. This era of rapid technological innovation transformed communication, commerce, and daily life. It also raised new ethical and philosophical questions about privacy, identity, and the nature of reality. The Digital Revolution has redefined human history in ways that were once unimaginable.

The invention of the transistor in the late 1940s paved the way for the development of modern computers. These early machines, initially used for military and scientific purposes, eventually found their way into businesses and homes. The rise of personal computers in the 1980s democratized access to information and technology, empowering individuals to create, learn, and connect in new ways. Companies like Apple and Microsoft played pivotal roles in popularizing personal computing, making technology an integral part of daily life.

The internet, initially developed as a research project by the U.S. Department of Defense, evolved into a global network that revolutionized communication. The World Wide Web, invented by Tim Berners-Lee in 1989, enabled the easy sharing and accessing of information through hyperlinks. The proliferation of websites, search engines, and online services transformed how people consumed information, conducted business, and interacted with one another. The rise of social media platforms, such as Facebook, Twitter, and Instagram, further revolutionized communication, creating new ways for people to connect and share their lives.

The Digital Revolution also gave rise to the information economy. E-commerce platforms like Amazon and eBay transformed retail, making it possible to buy and sell goods and services online. Digital payment systems, such as PayPal and cryptocurrencies, revolutionized financial transactions, providing new ways to transfer and store value. The gig economy, powered by platforms like Uber and Airbnb, redefined traditional notions of work and employment, offering new opportunities and challenges.

However, the Digital Revolution also raised important ethical and philosophical questions. The collection and use of personal data by tech companies sparked debates about privacy and surveillance. The rise of artificial intelligence and automation raised concerns about job displacement and the ethical implications of autonomous systems. The digital divide, the gap between those with access to technology and those without, highlighted issues of equity and inclusion. Furthermore, the spread of misinformation and the impact of digital technologies on mental health and social interactions became pressing concerns.

The Digital Revolution has fundamentally transformed human society, creating new opportunities and challenges. The integration of digital technologies into every aspect of life has reshaped how we communicate, work, and relate to one another. As we navigate this rapidly changing landscape, it is essential to consider the ethical and philosophical implications of technological advancements and strive to create a more just and equitable digital future.

8

Chapter 8: Artificial Intelligence

Artificial intelligence (AI) represents the next frontier of human innovation. As machines become increasingly capable of performing complex tasks, the line between human and machine blurs. This raises profound questions about consciousness, ethics, and the future of humanity. The development and deployment of AI have the potential to redefine our world in ways that were once the realm of science fiction.

The field of AI has its roots in the mid-20th century, with pioneers like Alan Turing and John McCarthy laying the theoretical groundwork. Turing's concept of a "universal machine" and his development of the Turing Test set the stage for the exploration of machine intelligence. McCarthy's coining of the term "artificial intelligence" and his contributions to the development of programming languages and AI algorithms were instrumental in advancing the field.

In recent decades, AI has made significant strides, driven by advancements in computing power, data availability, and machine learning techniques. Machine learning, a subset of AI, involves training algorithms to recognize patterns in data and make predictions or decisions based on that data. This approach has led to breakthroughs in various applications, from natural language processing and computer vision to autonomous vehicles and medical diagnostics.

One of the most prominent examples of AI is the development of neural networks and deep learning. These techniques, inspired by the structure and function of the human brain, have enabled machines to achieve remarkable levels of performance in tasks such as image recognition and language translation. AI systems like IBM's Watson, Google's AlphaGo, and OpenAI's GPT-3 have demonstrated the potential of AI to tackle complex problems and outperform human experts in specific domains.

The rise of AI also raises important ethical and philosophical questions. As machines become more capable, the potential for job displacement and economic disruption becomes a pressing concern. The development of autonomous systems, such as self-driving cars and drones, raises questions about accountability and decision-making in situations involving life and death. The use of AI in surveillance and law enforcement raises concerns about privacy, bias, and discrimination.

Furthermore, the prospect of achieving artificial general intelligence (AGI) – machines that possess human-like cognitive abilities – challenges our understanding of consciousness and the nature of intelligence. The possibility of creating sentient machines raises profound questions about the rights and responsibilities of AI entities and the ethical implications of creating beings with the capacity for independent thought and experience.

Artificial intelligence has the potential to transform every aspect of human life, from healthcare and education to transportation and entertainment. As we continue to develop and integrate AI technologies, it is crucial to consider the ethical and philosophical implications and strive to create a future where AI benefits all of humanity.

9

Chapter 9: Biotechnology

Biotechnology holds the promise of revolutionizing medicine and extending human life. From genetic engineering to regenerative medicine, these advancements challenge our understanding of life and mortality. The fusion of biology and technology has opened new frontiers in healthcare, agriculture, and environmental sustainability, reshaping our future in profound ways.

Genetic engineering is one of the most transformative fields within biotechnology. The discovery of the structure of DNA by James Watson and Francis Crick in 1953 laid the foundation for understanding the genetic code. This breakthrough led to the development of techniques for manipulating genes, enabling scientists to modify organisms at the molecular level. The advent of CRISPR-Cas9, a powerful gene-editing tool, has revolutionized genetic engineering by allowing precise and targeted modifications to DNA. This technology holds the potential to cure genetic disorders, enhance crop yields, and combat diseases such as cancer and HIV.

Regenerative medicine is another exciting area of biotechnology that focuses on repairing or replacing damaged tissues and organs. Stem cell research has shown promise in regenerating tissues and treating conditions such as spinal cord injuries, heart disease, and neurodegenerative disorders. Scientists are also exploring the potential of 3D bioprinting to create custom tissues and organs for transplantation. These advancements could one day eliminate the need for organ donors and revolutionize the field of transplantation.

Biotechnology also has significant implications for agriculture and food production. Genetically modified organisms (GMOs) have been developed to increase crop resilience, improve nutritional content, and reduce the need for chemical pesticides. These innovations have the potential to address food security challenges and support sustainable farming practices. Additionally, advances in biotechnology have led to the development of lab-grown meat and alternative protein sources, offering environmentally friendly solutions to meet the growing demand for food.

The rapid progress in biotechnology raises important ethical and philosophical questions. The ability to manipulate the genetic code and create new forms of life challenges our understanding of what it means to be human. Issues such as genetic privacy, the potential for designer babies, and the unintended consequences of genetic modifications require careful consideration. The ethical implications of cloning, stem cell research, and the use of animals in biotechnology are also subjects of ongoing debate.

As biotechnology continues to advance, it is essential to navigate the ethical and philosophical dilemmas it presents. The potential benefits of these technologies are immense, but so are the risks and uncertainties. By fostering a responsible and inclusive approach to biotechnology, we can harness its potential to improve human health, enhance food security, and promote environmental sustainability.

10

Chapter 10: Space Exploration

The quest to explore the cosmos has inspired generations of dreamers and scientists. Space exploration pushes the boundaries of human knowledge and raises fundamental questions about our place in the universe. The exploration of space has the potential to redefine our understanding of existence and inspire new technological advancements.

The journey to space began with the launch of the first artificial satellite, Sputnik, by the Soviet Union in 1957. This milestone marked the beginning of the space race and ignited a wave of technological innovation. In 1961, Yuri Gagarin became the first human to orbit the Earth, opening a new chapter in human history. The United States achieved a major milestone in 1969 when NASA's Apollo 11 mission successfully landed astronauts Neil Armstrong and Buzz Aldrin on the moon. Armstrong's iconic words, "That's one small step for man, one giant leap for mankind," captured the significance of this achievement and the boundless possibilities of space exploration.

The success of the Apollo missions paved the way for further exploration of the solar system. Robotic missions, such as the Mars rovers and the Voyager probes, have provided valuable insights into the geology, climate, and potential for life on other planets. The Hubble Space Telescope has revolutionized our understanding of the universe, capturing stunning images of distant galaxies, nebulae, and black holes. These missions have expanded our knowledge of the cosmos and inspired new generations of scientists and engineers.

In recent years, private companies have become key players in space exploration. Companies like SpaceX, Blue Origin, and Virgin Galactic are developing new technologies and ambitious plans for space travel. SpaceX's reusable rockets and the successful launch of the Crew Dragon spacecraft have demonstrated the potential for commercial spaceflight and the possibility of human missions to Mars. The development of space tourism and plans for lunar bases and Mars colonization reflect humanity's enduring fascination with the cosmos.

Space exploration also raises important philosophical and ethical questions. The search for extraterrestrial life challenges our understanding of life's uniqueness and the potential for other intelligent beings in the universe. The ethical implications of colonizing other planets and the responsible use of space resources require careful consideration. The vastness of space and the potential for interstellar travel also prompt reflections on the future of humanity and our place in the cosmos.

The quest to explore space is a testament to human curiosity, ingenuity, and the desire to push the boundaries of what is possible. As we continue to explore the cosmos, we must consider the ethical and philosophical implications of our endeavors and strive to ensure that space exploration benefits all of humanity.

11

Chapter 11: Environmental Philosophy

The growing awareness of environmental issues has given rise to new philosophical perspectives. These ideas challenge us to reconsider our relationship with the natural world and our responsibility to future generations. Environmental philosophy seeks to address the ethical, moral, and existential questions that arise from our interaction with the environment and the impact of human activities on the planet.

One of the foundational concepts in environmental philosophy is the idea of intrinsic value. This perspective argues that nature has inherent worth beyond its utility to humans. Environmental philosopher Aldo Leopold, in his seminal work "A Sand County Almanac," introduced the concept of the land ethic. Leopold's land ethic posits that humans are part of a larger ecological community and have a moral obligation to respect and care for the land. This idea challenges the anthropocentric view that nature exists solely for human exploitation and emphasizes the importance of ecological sustainability.

Deep ecology, another influential environmental philosophy, advocates for a profound shift in human consciousness and values. Coined by Norwegian philosopher Arne Naess, deep ecology calls for an ecological egalitarianism that recognizes the intrinsic worth of all living beings and ecosystems. It emphasizes the interconnectedness of all life forms and promotes a sense of humility and responsibility towards the natural world. Deep ecology critiques the dominant industrial and consumerist culture, advocating for a more sustainable and harmonious way of living.

Ecofeminism is a philosophical perspective that explores the connections between the exploitation of nature and the oppression of women. Ecofeminists argue that the patriarchal structures that marginalize women are similar to those that degrade the environment. Thinkers like Vandana Shiva and Karen Warren have highlighted the ways in which ecological degradation disproportionately affects women and marginalized communities. Ecofeminism calls for a more inclusive and just approach to environmental issues, recognizing the intersectionality of social and ecological justice.

The concept of environmental justice addresses the ethical and political dimensions of environmental issues. It examines the distribution of environmental benefits and burdens, advocating for the fair treatment and meaningful involvement of all people in environmental decision-making. Environmental justice movements have emerged to address issues such as pollution, climate change, and access to natural resources, emphasizing the need for equitable solutions that consider the rights and needs of vulnerable communities.

As the global environmental crisis intensifies, the importance of environmental philosophy becomes increasingly evident. The challenges of climate change, biodiversity loss, and resource depletion require not only technological solutions but also a fundamental rethinking of our values and ethical responsibilities. Environmental philosophy provides a framework for addressing these complex issues and guiding humanity towards a more sustainable and compassionate relationship with the natural world.

12

Chapter 12: Transhumanism

Transhumanism envisions a future where humans transcend their biological limitations through technology. This movement raises profound questions about identity, ethics, and the nature of humanity. Transhumanists advocate for the use of advanced technologies to enhance human abilities, extend lifespan, and improve the human condition, envisioning a future where humans and machines merge in new and transformative ways.

The concept of transhumanism can be traced back to the early 20th century, with thinkers like J.B.S. Haldane and Julian Huxley exploring the potential of science and technology to overcome human limitations. Huxley, who coined the term "transhumanism," believed that humanity's evolutionary journey was not complete and that we could take an active role in shaping our future. This idea laid the groundwork for the modern transhumanist movement, which emerged in the late 20th century with the advent of new technologies and scientific advancements.

One of the central goals of transhumanism is to extend human lifespan and achieve radical life extension. Advances in biotechnology, such as genetic engineering, regenerative medicine, and nanotechnology, hold the potential to slow down or even reverse the aging process. Researchers are exploring ways to repair cellular damage, replace worn-out tissues, and enhance the body's natural regenerative abilities. The prospect of significantly extending human life raises ethical questions about the implications for society, resource allocation, and the meaning of mortality.

Another key aspect of transhumanism is the enhancement of human cognitive and physical abilities. Neurotechnology, including brain-computer interfaces and cognitive enhancements, aims to augment human intelligence and improve mental functions. This could lead to breakthroughs in learning, memory, and problem-solving abilities. Similarly, advancements in robotics and cybernetics offer the potential for physical augmentation, enabling individuals to overcome disabilities or achieve superhuman capabilities. The integration of human and machine elements challenges traditional notions of identity and prompts reflections on what it means to be human.

Transhumanism also envisions a future where humans can transcend their physical bodies entirely. The concept of mind uploading, or transferring human consciousness to a digital substrate, has captured the imagination of many futurists. This idea raises questions about the nature of consciousness, the possibility of digital immortality, and the ethical implications of creating digital copies of human minds. The pursuit of such radical technologies prompts philosophical inquiries into the essence of personal identity and the boundaries between the biological and the digital.

While transhumanism offers a vision of enhanced human capabilities and extended lifespans, it also raises important ethical and societal concerns. The potential for inequality and access to enhancement technologies, the risk of unintended consequences, and the impact on social structures and relationships are critical issues that require careful consideration. As humanity embarks on this transformative journey, it is essential to engage in thoughtful and inclusive discussions about the ethical implications and strive to ensure that the benefits of transhumanism are accessible to all.

13

Chapter 13: The Philosophy of Technology

The philosophy of technology examines the relationship between humans and their creations. It explores how technology shapes our lives, identities, and societies. This field of philosophy addresses fundamental questions about the nature of technology, its ethical implications, and its impact on human existence. The philosophy of technology provides a framework for understanding the complex and dynamic interplay between humans and the tools they create.

One of the central themes in the philosophy of technology is the concept of technological determinism. This perspective argues that technology is the primary driver of societal change and that human choices and actions are shaped by technological developments. Thinkers like Marshall McLuhan and Jacques Ellul have explored the ways in which technology influences culture, communication, and social structures. McLuhan's famous phrase "the medium is the message" highlights the idea that the medium through which information is conveyed shapes our perceptions and experiences. Ellul's work, on the other hand, emphasizes the ways in which technological systems can become autonomous and shape human behavior in unintended ways.

Another important theme in the philosophy of technology is the idea of the "technological fix." This concept refers to the belief that technological solutions can address social, environmental, and ethical problems. While technological innovations have undoubtedly brought about significant improvements in various fields, the reliance on technological fixes raises questions about their long-term effectiveness and potential unintended consequences. Philosophers like Langdon Winner and Andrew Feenberg have critiqued the notion of the technological fix, arguing that it often overlooks the underlying social and political issues that contribute to the problems being addressed.

The philosophy of technology also examines the ethical implications of technological advancements. Issues such as privacy, surveillance, and the impact of digital technologies on human relationships are central to this field. The development of artificial intelligence, biotechnology, and other cutting-edge technologies raises new ethical dilemmas that require careful consideration. The concept of "responsible innovation" emphasizes the importance of anticipating and addressing the potential risks and ethical concerns associated with new technologies. This approach advocates for the involvement of diverse stakeholders in the decision-making process to ensure that technological advancements align with societal values and contribute to the common good.

The impact of technology on human identity and agency is another key area of exploration in the philosophy of technology. The integration of digital technologies into daily life has transformed how people perceive themselves and interact with others. The rise of social media, virtual reality, and wearable technologies raises questions about the nature of selfhood and the boundaries between the physical and digital worlds. Philosophers like Don Ihde and Sherry Turkle have explored the ways in which technology mediates human experiences and shapes our sense of identity and autonomy.

The philosophy of technology provides valuable insights into the ways in which technology influences human life and society. By examining the ethical, social, and existential implications of technological advancements, this field of philosophy helps us navigate the complex and ever-changing technological landscape. As we continue to innovate and create new technologies, it is essential to engage in thoughtful and critical reflection on their impact and

CHAPTER 13: THE PHILOSOPHY OF TECHNOLOGY

strive to ensure that they contribute to human flourishing.

14

Chapter 14: The Future of Human Thought

As we look to the future, the interplay between philosophy and technology will continue to shape our world. Emerging technologies and new philosophical ideas will challenge us to rethink what it means to be human. The future of human thought will be defined by our ability to navigate the ethical, social, and existential implications of technological advancements and to harness their potential for the betterment of humanity.

One of the most promising areas of future technological development is artificial intelligence. As AI systems become more sophisticated, they will have the potential to augment human intelligence and creativity. The development of artificial general intelligence (AGI) could lead to breakthroughs in fields such as medicine, environmental science, and education. However, the pursuit of AGI also raises profound ethical and existential questions about the nature of consciousness, the potential for machine autonomy, and the implications for human identity and agency.

The field of biotechnology will continue to advance, offering new possibilities for enhancing human health and extending lifespan. Advances in genetic engineering, regenerative medicine, and personalized medicine hold the potential to revolutionize healthcare and improve quality of life.

CHAPTER 14: THE FUTURE OF HUMAN THOUGHT

The ethical considerations surrounding these technologies, such as genetic privacy, the potential for designer babies, and the equitable distribution of medical advancements, will be critical areas of philosophical inquiry.

Space exploration and the potential colonization of other planets will also shape the future of human thought. The quest to explore the cosmos and the search for extraterrestrial life challenge our understanding of existence and our place in the universe. The ethical implications of space exploration, such as the potential for environmental impact and the responsible use of space resources, will require careful consideration. The prospect of interstellar travel and the possibility of encountering other intelligent beings will prompt new philosophical reflections on the nature of life and consciousness.

The integration of digital technologies into every aspect of life will continue to transform human society. The rise of the Internet of Things (IoT), augmented reality (AR), and virtual reality (VR) will create new ways of interacting with the world and with each other. These technologies will raise questions about privacy, security, and the nature of human experience. The development of brain-computer interfaces and neurotechnology will challenge our understanding of the mind and the boundaries between the biological and the digital.

As we navigate the future, the interplay between philosophy and technology will be essential in addressing the complex and multifaceted challenges that arise. The future of human thought will be defined by our ability to engage in critical reflection, ethical deliberation, and creative problem-solving. By fostering a responsible and inclusive approach to technological innovation, we can harness the potential of these advancements to create a more just, equitable, and sustainable world.

15

Chapter 15: Conclusion: The Mind's Machine

In the final chapter, we will reflect on the journey of human thought and innovation. From ancient philosophy to cutting-edge technology, the interplay between ideas and inventions has redefined our world. The Mind's Machine has been driven by the relentless pursuit of knowledge, the desire to understand existence, and the quest to improve the human condition.

Throughout history, philosophy and technology have shaped each other in profound ways. The earliest contemplations of existence laid the groundwork for the development of language, science, and ethical systems. The great philosophers of antiquity explored fundamental questions about reality, ethics, and society, laying the intellectual foundation for future generations. The Renaissance and the Enlightenment brought about a cultural and intellectual awakening, fueling advancements in art, science, and politics.

The Industrial Revolution and the Digital Revolution transformed human society, creating new opportunities and challenges. Technological advancements have improved quality of life, increased productivity, and connected the world in unprecedented ways. However, they have also raised important ethical and philosophical questions about privacy, equity, and the impact on human relationships and the environment.

CHAPTER 15: CONCLUSION: THE MIND'S MACHINE

The rise of artificial intelligence, biotechnology, and space exploration offers new possibilities for enhancing human capabilities and understanding the cosmos. These advancements challenge our understanding of what it means to be human and prompt reflections on the ethical implications of our creations. As we navigate the future, the interplay between philosophy and technology will continue to shape our world, guiding us towards a more just, equitable, and sustainable future.

The Mind's Machine is a testament to the power of human thought and innovation. It reflects our enduring curiosity, creativity, and resilience in the face of challenges. By embracing the ethical and philosophical dimensions of technological advancements, we can harness their potential to improve the human condition and create a better world for future generations.

Book Description: The Mind's Machine: How Philosophy and Technology Have Redefined Human History

The Mind's Machine is a captivating exploration of the intertwined evolution of human thought and technological innovation. This book delves into the profound ways in which philosophy and technology have shaped the course of human history, from the earliest days of contemplative thought to the cutting-edge advancements of the digital age.

The journey begins with the dawn of human cognition, tracing the development of language and early philosophical ideas that laid the foundation for future intellectual pursuits. Readers will encounter the great minds of ancient Greece and China, whose teachings on ethics, politics, and the cosmos have left an indelible mark on human thought.

As the narrative progresses, the book examines pivotal moments in history, such as the Renaissance and the Enlightenment, where the fusion of classical wisdom and scientific discoveries redefined human potential. The Industrial Revolution and the Digital Revolution are explored in detail, highlighting the transformative impact of technological advancements on society, economy, and daily life.

The book also delves into contemporary and future-oriented topics, including artificial intelligence, biotechnology, and space exploration. It raises profound ethical and philosophical questions about the nature of consciousness, the potential for life extension, and humanity's place in the universe. Environmental philosophy and transhumanism are examined, challenging readers to reconsider their relationship with the natural world and the ethical implications of transcending biological limitations.

The Mind's Machine offers a comprehensive and thought-provoking narrative that weaves together the threads of philosophy and technology. It invites readers to reflect on the ethical, social, and existential implications of technological advancements and to consider the future trajectories of human thought and innovation. This book is a testament to the power of human curiosity, creativity, and resilience in shaping the world we live in and envisioning a better future for all.

www.ingramcontent.com/pod-product-compliance
Lightning Source LLC
LaVergne TN
LVHW020501080526
838202LV00057B/6084